CAN THE WORLD TOLERATE AN IRAN WITH NUCLEAR WEAPONS?

CAN THE WORLD TOLERATE AN IRAN WITH NUCLEAR WEAPONS?

KRAUTHAMMER AND YADLIN VS. ZAKARIA AND NASR

THE MUNK DEBATE ON IRAN

Edited by Rudyard Griffiths

ANANSI

This edition published in 2013 by
House of Anansi Press Inc.
110 Spadina Avenue, Suite 801
Toronto, ON, M5V 2K4
Tel. 416-363-4343
Fax 416-363-1017
www.houseofanansi.com

Distributed in Canada by
HarperCollins Canada Ltd.
1995 Markham Road
Scarborough, ON, M1B 5M8
Toll free tel. 1-800-387-0117

Distributed in the United States by
Publishers Group West
1700 Fourth Street
Berkeley, CA 94710
Toll free tel. 1-800-788-3123

The transcript of this debate seeks to be as close to a verbatim account of its proceedings as possible. Every reasonable effort has been made to verify the accuracy of the facts and statistics presented in this debate.

House of Anansi Press is committed to protecting our natural environment. As part of our efforts, the interior of this book is printed on paper that contains 100% post-consumer recycled fibres, is acid-free, and is processed chlorine-free.

17 16 15 14 13   1 2 3 4 5

Library and Archives Canada Cataloguing in Publication

Can the world tolerate an Iran with nuclear weapons? : the Munk debate
on Iran / Amos Yadlin . . . [et al.] ; Rudyard
Griffiths, editor.

(The Munk debates)
Issued also in electronic format.
ISBN: 978-1-77089-236-1

1. Nuclear weapons — Iran. 2. Iran — Strategic aspects.
3. Iran — Military policy. 4. Security, International.
I. Yadlin, Amos 1951–
II. Griffiths, Rudyard III. Series: Munk debates

U264.5I7C36 2012   355.02'170955   C2012-907356-3

Library of Congress Control Number: 2012952631

Cover design: Alysia Shewchuk
Text design and typesetting: Colleen Wormald
Transcription: Rondi Adamson

*We acknowledge for their financial support of our publishing program
the Canada Council for the Arts, the Ontario Arts Council, and the Government of Canada
through the Canada Book Fund.*

Printed and bound in Canada

CONTENTS

FOREWORD BY PETER MUNK

Since we started the Munk Debates, my wife Melanie and I have been deeply gratified at how quickly they have captured the public's imagination. From the time of our first event in May 2008, we have been able to host what I believe are some of the most exciting public policy debates in Canada and internationally. Global in focus, the Munk Debates have tackled a range of issues such as humanitarian intervention, the effectiveness of foreign aid, the threat of global warming, religion's impact on geopolitics, the rise of China, and the decline of Europe. These compelling topics have served as the intellectual and ethical grist for some of the world's most important thinkers and doers from Henry Kissinger to Tony Blair to Christopher Hitchens to Paul Krugman to Lord Peter Mandelson to Fareed Zakaria.

Let me say a few words about why we started this program and why we believe so strongly that the Munk

Debates originate out of Toronto, Canada. As a Canadian who wasn't born in this country, a country that has accepted me with open arms and provided me with endless opportunities, I believe strongly that Canada must be a vital participant in world affairs. That was the primary reason that Melanie and I helped found the Munk School of Global Affairs at the University of Toronto, my alma mater. It was the same thinking that led my Aurea Foundation to launch the Munk Debates. We wanted to create a forum that attracts the best minds and debaters to address some of the most important international issues of our time, and make these debates available to the widest possible audience. And we wanted Toronto to be at the centre of this international dialogue to affirm Canada's growing role as a world economic, intellectual, and moral leader.

Melanie and I are extremely gratified that the Munk Debates are making significant strides toward fulfilling the mission and spirit of our philanthropy. The issues raised at the debates have not only fostered public awareness, they have helped all of us become more involved and therefore less intimidated by the concept of globalization. It's so easy to be inward-looking. It's so easy to be xenophobic. It's so easy to be nationalistic. The hard thing is to go into the unknown. Globalization, to many people, is an abstract concept at best. These debates are meant to encourage us to further engagement with the forces, good and bad, of globalization and the ancillary geopolitical issues that define our era in human history. The purpose of this debate series is to help people feel more familiar with our fast-changing world, and more comfortable participating in the global dialogue about the issues and events that will shape our collective future. It is essential today that we equip ourselves, and especially young people, with the skills and inclination to become vital and engaged participants in global affairs.

I don't need to tell you that there are many, many burning issues. Whether you talk about global warming or the plight of extreme poverty, whether you talk about genocide or whether you talk about our shaky global financial order, there are many critical issues that matter to many people. And it seems to me, and to the Aurea Foundation board members, that the quality of the public dialogue on these critical issues diminishes in direct proportion to the importance and the number of these issues clamouring for our attention. By trying to highlight the most important issues at crucial moments in the global conversation, these debates not only profile the ideas and solutions of some of our brightest thinkers and doers, but crystallize public passion and knowledge, helping to tackle some global challenges confronting humankind. Just as important, they seek to make Canada the forum where Canadians and the international community can observe world-class thinkers engage each other on the big issues of the day.

I learned in life — and I'm sure many of you will share this view — that challenges bring out the best in us. I hope you'll also agree that the participants in these debates challenge not only each other, but they challenge us to think clearly and logically about important problems facing the world.

Peter Munk
Founder, the Aurea Foundation
Toronto, Ontario

INTRODUCTION BY RUDYARD GRIFFITHS

Great debates occur when you get the right speakers, talking about the right issues, at the right time. On all three counts our contest on Iran's nuclear ambitions exceeded expectations. Arguing for the motion "Be it resolved, the world cannot tolerate an Iran with nuclear weapons capability," was the formidable team of Charles Krauthammer and Maj. Gen. (ret.) Amos Yadlin. Recently celebrated by the *Financial Times* as America's most influential political commentator, Charles Krauthammer is renowned for his steely analysis and take-no-prisoners approach to public debate. He is the author of a highly respected *Washington Post* column on U.S. domestic and international politics, which is syndicated in over 275 newspapers worldwide. He is also a contributing editor to *The Weekly Standard* and *The New Republic*, and a closely followed political commentator for Fox News in America.

While Charles Krauthammer's debating partner is less well known to Western audiences, he is a household name in his native country of Israel. Retired from the Israel Defense Forces, Maj. Gen. (ret.) Amos Yadlin's military career is synonymous with the nuclear threats that have confronted the Jewish homeland. In 1981, he was one of the eight pilots who strapped themselves into F-16 fighters and successfully bombed the Osirak reactor in Iraq. Later, in 2007, as head of Military Intelligence for the IDF, he helped lead the campaign that demolished Syria's Deir ez-Zor reactor. As a national security adviser up until 2011, he played a key role in managing Israel's overt and covert campaign against Iran's uranium enrichment program. Today, he leads the prestigious Institute for National Security Studies at Tel Aviv University and writes and speaks widely on national security issues.

One superstar team of debaters deserves another. In Vali Nasr and Fareed Zakaria we were fortunate to have recruited a policy duo who could make the case for why the world *can* tolerate an Iran with nuclear weapons capability *and* match the formidable expertise and rhetorical savvy of Krauthammer and Yadlin.

Vali Nasr is dean of Johns Hopkins University's renowned Paul H. Nitze School of Advanced International Studies. Born in Tehran, Dean Nasr is one of the world's top experts on the politics and social development of the Middle East and Iran and is the author of the highly respected books *The Shia Revival* and *Democracy in Iran.* He is also a distinguished public servant. From 2009 to

2011 he held the post of senior adviser to the U.S. special representative for Afghanistan and Pakistan, the late Richard Holbrooke, and he currently sits on the U.S. State Department's Foreign Policy Advisory Board. As a critic of the Iranian regime's human rights record and acts of political oppression, Vali Nasr brought an invaluable and authentic Iranian perspective to the debate.

Fareed Zakaria is known internationally as the host of CNN's flagship global affairs program, *Fareed Zakaria GPS*, which airs in over 200 countries worldwide. He is also a celebrated *Washington Post* columnist and the editor-at-large of *Time* magazine. The author of four bestselling books on geopolitics, including *The Post-American World: Release 2.0*, Dr. Zakaria was recently ranked by *Foreign Policy* magazine as one of the world's top twenty thinkers on international affairs. As revealed in the transcript of the debate, Zakaria's CNN media experience stood him in good stead when going up against a trenchant Charles Krauthammer. The CNN versus Fox News dynamic of the debate only added to the tension on the stage.

As important as experienced and knowledgeable debaters are to creating a battle of the wits and brainpower, good debates are separated from great debates by the issues that animate them and their importance to public conversation as a whole.

It is hard to think of a global issue today that is as potent and complex as Iran's nuclear enrichment program. For commentators such as Yadlin and

Krauthammer, the case to prevent Iran's acquisition of nuclear weapons capability is ironclad. For starters, both see a nuclear-armed Iran as dangerously destabilizing a Middle East already roiled by the Arab Spring. Specifically, Yadlin and Krauthammer see the emergence of a Persian bomb as supercharging Shia–Sunni conflicts throughout the region as the Gulf States and Egypt rush to secure their own nuclear weapons to thwart Iran's bid for regional supremacy. And an Iran with nuclear weapons capability clearly has the potential to raise already heightened tensions with Israel to the level of armed conflict.

Critics of Iran's nuclear ambitions, such as Yadlin and Krauthammer, rightly ask: How can the Jewish homeland, with its unique history and the lessons of the Holocaust, be expected to co-exist with a nuclear-armed state whose leadership has called for Israel's destruction? At one particularly powerful moment in the debate, Amos Yadlin reminded the audience: "It is much more frightening to have a real gun barrel pointed directly at your face than watching it on CNN or reading about it in the *Washington Post.* Last week, Israel was showered with 1,500 rockets and missiles from Gaza, aimed at innocent Israelis . . . Iranian rockets and missiles that were supplied to Hamas and jihadists . . . Thank God they were not nuclear missiles."

Also, beyond destabilizing the already fraught power dynamics of the Middle East, what would an Iran with an atomic bomb say about the international community's multi-decade effort to limit the spread of nuclear weapons? For Krauthammer, failure to prevent an Iranian bomb — just a few short years after North Korea successfully detonated nuclear devices — risks ushering in an era of hyper-proliferation where powers large and small believe their security can only be guaranteed by having nuclear weapons. For staunch opponents of a nuclear-armed Iran, such as Yadlin and Krauthammer, one can draw a straight line through history from the bombing of Hiroshima and Nagasaki to the advent of an Iranian nuclear device to the inevitable use of nuclear weapons in our own lifetime.

But are these kinds of alarming prognostications the only way to assess the impact of an Iran with nuclear weapons capability? Over the course of this gripping two-hour debate, Nasr and Zakaria advanced a number of powerful counter-arguments, which, taken together, built an equally compelling case for why the world might well find itself able to live with a nuclear-armed Iran.

To contradict the claim that an Iran with nuclear weapons would plunge the Middle East into a regional arms race and fuel intercommunal conflict among Muslims, Nasr and Zakaria evoked the traditional arguments of nuclear deterrence. Proponents of deterrence theory, such as Nasr and Zakaria, believe that a nuclear Iran, as well as the other powers in the region the country could conceivably threaten, know that any unilateral use of atomic weapons would bring about an overwhelming global response, including the threat of a catastrophic nuclear counterstrike. According to this line of reasoning, the Iranian regime's quest for nuclear weapons capability is driven by its desire to increase its power and legitimacy domestically and within the larger Muslim world. Iran's nuclear ambitions are not the culmination of a diabolical plan to destroy Israel or wage wars of regional conquest.

Nasr and Zakaria point out that if Israel or the United States were to pre-emptively attack a nuclear-armed Iran, it would plunge the Middle East into chaos. And intelligence experts believe that a pre-emptive attack would only delay the regime's acquisition of weapons capability by two to three years at most. For both debaters there is no real choice between the limited effects of a pre-emptive attack carried out by the United States or Israel versus the immense status that such a strike would confer on the Iranian regime, both on its own people and on the larger Muslim world. Instead, Nasr and Zakaria counsel that the best and maybe only course Israel and the West could take to confront the threat of nuclear-armed Iran would be to mirror the way the United States managed nuclear-armed China and Russia or to adopt a long-term policy of containment and credible deterrence.

The most controversial argument in favour of the world learning to live with a nuclear-armed Iran is the contention that nuclear weapons deter armed conflict, full stop. The classic example of this for Zakaria is India and Pakistan, which fought bloody conventional wars up until, but not after, acquiring nuclear weapons. The logical extension of this proposition, advanced by Nasr and

Zakaria, is that for Iran, as well as Israel, the threat of conventional conflicts spiralling into nuclear war could just as easily lead to a period of Middle East détente as opposed to heightened conflict in the region. This highly contentious view featured prominently in our debate and fuelled some of its most lively and thought-provoking exchanges.

Great debates are not only defined by the weightiness of the issues they seek to illuminate; the state and play of global events are key to the drama and intensity they generate. As of the publication of this book, the Iranian regime continues to suffer under punitive international sanctions and a viselike oil embargo. The country maintains its plans to enrich its uranium stockpiles and thereby advance its ability to develop a nuclear weapon. The International Atomic Energy Agency has estimated, as recently as November 2012, that Iran will have enough enriched uranium of the requisite purity to move quickly to create an atomic bomb as early as June 2013. Whatever its ultimate intentions, how the world will respond to Iran crossing this "redline" will be one of the defining geopolitical events of our time.

All of us associated with the Munk Debates hope that this debate and the publication of its proceedings will provide the West, Israel, and the Middle East with a better understanding of the geopolitical implications of Iran developing nuclear weapons capability. How the world acts, should this moment come to pass in 2013 or beyond, will shape the course of history for the Middle East and its relationship to Israel and the West for a generation to come. And whether you agree or disagree that the world cannot tolerate an Iran with nuclear weapons capability, more debate of this issue, thoughtfully presented and cogently argued, can only help inform the global conversation the world needs to have.

Rudyard Griffiths
Moderator and Organizer, the Munk Debates
Toronto, Ontario

Be It Resolved the World Cannot Tolerate an Iran with Nuclear Weapons Capability

Pro: Charles Krauthammer and Amos Yadlin
Con: Fareed Zakaria and Vali Nasr

November 27, 2012
Toronto, Ontario

THE MUNK DEBATE ON IRAN

RUDYARD GRIFFITHS: Ladies and gentlemen, welcome to the Munk Debate on Iran's nuclear ambitions. My name is Rudyard Griffiths, and it is my privilege to organize this series with my colleague Patrick Luciani, and to once again act as your moderator.

Tonight is a special evening for this series — tonight we convene for our tenth semi-annual Munk Debate. As we enter our fifth year, we've hosted over thirty-eight speakers on the Munk Debate stage, leading thinkers such as Christopher Hitchens, Tony Blair, Henry Kissinger — who could forget him? — Paul Krugman, and Larry Summers. This debate series is undeniably making a lasting contribution to better public debate not only in Canada, but internationally. We're doing that through TV and radio broadcasts on the BBC, through our homegrown champions and supporters of this debate series, CBC Radio and the *Globe and Mail*, and through our unique publishing agreement with House of Anansi Press, which has made books of these debates for the North American market and helped see them translated into over a dozen languages and published throughout the world. It is, therefore, unquestionable that this series is having an international impact.

But the success of this debate series is really thanks to you, the 3,000 people here at Roy Thomson Hall tonight, and to the thousands more watching online, who represent our 30,000-strong membership. Furthermore, all of this would not be possible without two other very special people. Ladies and gentlemen, please join me in a big round of applause for our hosts and originators of this debate series, Peter and Melanie Munk of the Aurea Foundation. Bravo.

Now, the moment we've all been waiting for: let's get our two teams of powerhouse debaters out onto the stage and get our contest underway. Arguing for the motion, "Be it resolved, the world cannot tolerate an Iran with nuclear weapons capability," are Charles Krauthammer and Maj. Gen. (ret.) Amos Yadlin.

Since tonight is an anniversary of sorts for the Munk Debates, who better to have on stage than Charles Krauthammer, a debater from the winning team of our very first debate in 2008? He writes a must-read column in the *Washington Post* on U.S. and international politics, which is syndicated in over 275 newspapers around the world. His acerbic analysis and his steely reputation on

Fox News for not suffering fools gladly have made him one of America's most influential commentators.

Given recent events in the Middle East, we are very fortunate to host Amos Yadlin as Charles's debating partner. His career in the Israel Defense Forces was synonymous with the nuclear threats that have confronted his country; highlights include being one of eight F-16 pilots to strap themselves into jets and destroy the Osirak reactor in Iraq in 1981, to up until a few years ago playing a key role in managing Israel's overt and covert campaign against Iran's nuclear enrichment program.

Now, let's get out on the stage the equally formidable duo who will be arguing against tonight's resolution, Vali Nasr and Fareed Zakaria. Dean Vali Nasr leads Johns Hopkins University's prestigious School of Advanced International Studies. Born in Tehran, he is one of the world's top experts on the political and social development of Iran. He is also the author of two bestselling books, *The Shia Revival* and *Democracy in Iran*. He sits on the State Department's influential Foreign Policy Advisory Board and, as recently as 2011, served as senior adviser for Afghanistan and Pakistan to the late Richard Holbrooke, a former Munk debater.

When you think of provocative conversation on the big foreign policy challenges of the day, you have to think about our next debater, Fareed Zakaria. His flagship global affairs program on CNN is seen in over 200 countries worldwide, but he is anything but a talking head on cable TV. He writes a highly respected column for the *Washington Post* and is the editor-at-large of *Time* magazine. His numerous bestselling books include *The Post-American World* and *The Future of Freedom.*

Finally, before we kick off our debate, let's see how the 3,000 people gathered tonight in Roy Thomson Hall voted on our resolution. This is how things stood as you took your seats: 60 percent voted in favour of the motion, 24 percent were opposed, and 16 percent were undecided. We also asked you a second question: Are you open to changing your vote depending on what you hear during the debate? Let's see how many proverbial swing states we have in the audience this evening. Wow — that's different. Eighty-two percent of you would change your minds in the next hour and forty-five minutes. Only 18 percent of you have your minds completely made up. In past Munk Debates we've seen higher levels of potential voter changes, but this debate is still very much in play.

We are just moments from getting the debate under-way. Before we hear opening statements, I'm going to ask the audience for their assistance to ensure our debaters stay on time in terms of their opening and closing remarks, and to help keep the debate on track as the night goes on. You will notice this handy countdown clock on stage: when it reaches zero, please applaud. This will let our debaters know that the time is over for their opening and closing statements. It is now time for opening statements. Dr. Charles Krauthammer, you are up first.

CHARLES KRAUTHAMMER: Thank you for that kind introduction. There are nice introductions; there are kind introductions. The nice ones are where they list all of your achievements, they get a copy made and notarized, and they send it to your mother. The kind introductions are the ones where they leave stuff out. For example, I appreciate that you left out the fact that I once worked for the famously liberal Sen. Walter Mondale. People sometimes ask me, "How do you go from Walter Mondale to Fox News?" I tell them it's easy. I was young once.

Also, I appreciate the fact that you left out that I was once a psychiatrist. In fact, technically I still am a psychiatrist. But in reality I am a psychiatrist in remission, doing extremely well, thank you. I haven't had a relapse in twenty-five years. I'm sometimes asked to compare what I do now as a political analyst in Washington with what I did back when I was a psychiatrist in Boston, and I tell people that, as you can imagine, it is not that different. In both lines of work I deal with people every day who suffer from paranoia and delusions of grandeur. The only difference is that in Washington the paranoids have access to nuclear weapons, which makes the stakes a little higher, the work a little more interesting, and which leads us to tonight's debate.

Can we live with nuclear weapons in the hands of a regime like Iran's? The answer is no. I will give you three reasons why I think so, to start off the debate, and we'll get into the details as we go on. I'm sure you will enforce the six-minute rule.

I think we have to look at this in concentric circles of

decreasing size — the global, the regional, and the local effect. So the first reason is global. The global problem, or threat, is that the world has been, for sixty years, trying to curtail and prevent the spread of nuclear weapons. Hyper-proliferation is the ultimate world nightmare. We congratulated ourselves when Brazil and Argentina renounced nuclear weapons. Imagine what the world would be like if Iran, the most important, the most powerful, the most aggressive and — according to the State Department — the greatest exporter of terror in the world, and the most aggressive and radical state in the Middle East, were to acquire nuclear weapons. That would be the end of non-proliferation. Do you think the weaker nations in the region are going to take refuge in the parchment of the Treaty on the Non-Proliferation of Nuclear Weapons (NPT)? No.

Here is what will happen: "Uncontrollable nuclear proliferation throughout a region roiled by revolution and sectarian blood feuds." Those are the words of Henry Kissinger, who knows something about deterrence, both when it works and when it doesn't. We will get an instant nuclear arms race. All the important neighbours — Saudi Arabia, Egypt, Turkey, and Syria — will join in. Think of Syria. God knows who will be in charge of Syria in the future. All those countries will go nuclear, assuming that Iran goes nuclear first.

And it's not just in the immediate Middle East; this is going to spread in the region. Our opponents tonight are going to speak reassuringly about deterrence. But the experience that we have had with stable deterrence is in a bipolar system, when it was just the United States and the Soviet Union. Imagine what deterrence would look like with six, seven, eight powers — countries that are unstable, some revolutionary, and with shifting alliances. How do you enforce or rely on deterrence in those circumstances? You could get accidental or unauthorized use; you could have theft; you could allow deliberate proliferation in the hands of terrorists. Imagine what would have happened if al Qaeda had nukes on 9/11. If they got their hands on nuclear weapons now, would they hesitate for a second in using them in such an attack in the future? That is the threat; that is the end of non-proliferation and the end of world reliance on deterrence.

Second, we have always tried to prevent a hegemon rising in the Middle East, in control of the world's oil, in control of the strategically important region. That is why there was an Iraq war in 1991 over the invasion of Kuwait. What the Arabs understand in the region is that, once Iran is nuclear, it becomes the hegemon of the region — the most aggressive, radically Islamist, anti-Western state, in charge of the strategic area of the Middle East. That is why the Gulf states, in private, have beseeched the United States to take out the nuclear program in advance, and that is why the Saudis would line the desert with directional arrows saying, "This way to Tehran," if Israel were to ever attack Iran's nuclear facilities.

Now lastly, and I notice that I'm running out of time, so I hope perhaps you will desist from applauding at the six-minute mark, or at least the 60 percent of you who are sympathetic to our view will desist, and drown out the others. My final point is that this is a regime that has threatened to annihilate Israel and has expressed its intention to do so. We are told we have to rely on deterrence because it worked in the Cold War. The Cold War was radically different. The Soviets were engaged in an ideological argument with the United States. It was not existential. And the target, the United States, was a continental nation of great size. Israel is a one-bomb country.

[Audience applauds for the six-minute mark.] That's a very strong 23 percent. I commend you on your energy. I will stop here and say there is a radical difference between the Soviet-U.S. relationship and the relationship of Israel and Iran, and you will not ask six million Jews in Israel to rely for their existence on deterrence in this kind of situation. Thank you very much.

RUDYARD GRIFFITHS: Charles, if it makes you feel any better, Henry Kissinger didn't get away with going over the six-minute mark either. Up next is Dean Vali Nasr; the podium is yours.

VALI NASR: Good evening, and thank you for that introduction. It is a pleasure being here. Let me start by saying that it is clear that the world would be better off if Iran does not become a nuclear-armed state, and that achieving that goal should be our principal aim going forward. However, despite our best efforts, that undesirable end may very well come to pass.

Should we act as if this is the first time that we have encountered such a challenge, or that the logic of containment and deterrence somehow does not apply to Iran — that Iran is somehow to be set apart from the realm of politics as we know it? The answer is no. As troublesome and menacing as Iran has been, its behaviour still reflects the pursuit of national interests. The country has a strategy, which it pursues, and in the course of doing so reacts to incentives and pressure. We don't approve of its methods, but we understand its goals. In short, Iran is a familiar problem, one with which we have plenty of experience.

During the Cold War, we managed peace and prosperity in Europe and Asia, containing both the nuclear-armed Soviet Union and China. We may parse details as to what the similarities and differences are in the Middle East, but the principle is very clear. We are still guaranteeing peace and prosperity in Asia by containing the very dangerous North Korean regime, which is armed with nuclear weapons and threatening to set Seoul on fire on a weekly basis. India, too, has been prospering, while tolerating great nuclear danger from a neighbouring country, which is known for its instability, adventurism, and support for terrorism. That situation has been going on for over two decades and yet there is a stable containment situation that has allowed the Indian economy to prosper.

It is often argued that Iran is different because the Iranian regime is irrational and messianic, to the point that it is impervious to the logic of containment and deterrence. It is assumed that Iran's singular aim is to start a nuclear Armageddon the minute that it acquires nuclear weapons, that it is actually religiously mandated to do so. But there are plenty of American politicians who believe in the Rapture, and that does not mean that you can read American foreign policy on the basis of that belief. If Iranians were truly driven by messianism in their foreign policy, they would have reacted when the shrine most directly associated with their hidden imam was blown up in Iraq in 2006, and yet they didn't. The last time Iran attacked a neighbour was in 1859, to reclaim Afghan territories that had been snatched away by Great Britain. The record of the past three decades shows that as objectionable and problematic as Iran's behaviour has been, it is still driven by the cold calculations of regime survival and national interests.

You don't need a degree in Islamic studies to understand Iranian strategy or to conclude that a regime that has managed to survive in power for three decades could not be suicidal or completely reckless. In fact, despite its bluster and support for terrorism, Iran has been more accepting of international norms than was ever the case with communist China, or is the case with North Korea, or even Pakistan. We talk about the proliferation issue, but let us remember, it was Pakistan — while in America's tight embrace — and not Iran, that began acting as a nuclear eBay.

If we are to say that we will not tolerate a nuclear Iran, then we have to basically say we are prepared to go down the path to war with Iran. We should ask ourselves: Could we tolerate another major war in the Middle East? This time it would be with a country that is twice as large and twice as populous as Iraq; it has a much larger land mass; and its capital city is 2,000 km and two mountain ranges away from the nearest port facilities. And we have to ask ourselves: Will that war actually be effective? Will it get the job done? How long would that war take? Five years? Ten years? Twenty years? Longer? How much will it cost? How many more trillions of dollars would this war cost the United States? How many Americans would die in such a war? Ten thousand? Fifteen thousand? More?

How would such a war impact the Middle East or America, for that matter? Do we want such a war? Can we tolerate it? It seems that the Americans have already answered this, from the president down. They have answered these questions very clearly and it is a resounding no. They don't want such a war. The good news is that they don't have to have it. If it becomes necessary, if the diplomatic efforts and the sanctions to stop Iran in its tracks were to fail, we can manage a nuclear Iran, just as we managed a nuclear Soviet Union, communist China, North Korea, and Pakistan. Thank you.

RUDYARD GRIFFITHS: Well, the debate is shaping up nicely. Next up is Amos Yadlin.

AMOS YADLIN: It is 2 a.m. in Tel Aviv, and I am the only one who does not speak English every day, so please be patient with me.

It is much more frightening to have a real gun barrel pointed directly at your face than watching it on CNN or reading about it in the *Washington Post*. Last week, Israel was showered with 1,500 rockets and missiles from Gaza, aimed at innocent Israelis — innocent citizens, women, and children. Those were Iranian rockets and missiles that were supplied to Hamas and jihadists in Gaza. Thank God they were not nuclear missiles.

Iranian leaders are the only country leaders calling for the destruction of a UN member state. Every day the supreme leader, the president, the chief of staff, use expressions like "annihilation," "cancer removal," and "wipe off the map" when they talk about Israel. Iranian leaders are also Holocaust deniers. Seventy years ago, our grandparents in Europe would have never imagined — in their wildest dreams — that Hitler intended to do exactly what he said to the Jews. I suggest that we take this current Iranian threat very, very seriously.

Why? Because Iran has a cruel and radical regime, regarding both internal and external issues. They publicly hang sixteen-year-old gays on cranes; they torture their own citizens and kill them in prison. Remember Zahra Kazemi, the Canadian photographer who was arrested, tortured, raped, and killed in Iranian prison in 2003? That is usual behaviour for this regime. They tamper with election results and crack down on the opposition. Iran is also the number one sponsor of state global terror, and has, for many years, exercised terror all over the world. They bombed, through Hezbollah, the U.S. embassy in Beirut in the '80s. They also killed more than 200 marines in their barracks in Beirut during the same decade. And in the '90s, they attacked and bombed the Israeli embassy and the Jewish community centre in Buenos Aires.

And what is the Iranian regime doing today? In Syria, they are supporting President Bashar al-Assad in killing more than 30,000 of his own citizens. This is a country that backs every negative regime in the world. Now imagine if Iran possessed nuclear weapons. Would these be passed on to terrorists, just as the best Iranian weapons have made their way to Hezbollah? Hezbollah is the only terrorist organization in the world with ballistic missiles and UAVs (unmanned aerial vehicles). What makes us sure they wouldn't get their hands on Iranian nuclear weapons?

But there is not only the terror aspect. A nuclear Iran will be the end of nuclear non-proliferation as we know it, and the Middle East would become even more unstable. Saudi Arabia is very worried; they are more concerned about a nuclear Iran than Israel. If Iran gets a nuclear weapon, the Saudis will go to Pakistan the next day for a bomb — they have already paid for it. Egypt, Turkey, Iraq — every country believed to be a regional superpower — will go nuclear. And a nuclear balance that includes many participants is not stable. Even if it is just Israel against Iran, the main concept of MAD (Mutual Assured Destruction), which basically stabilized the Cold War, will be non-existent. Remember that there is no hotline between Iran and Israel.

We are currently celebrating the fiftieth anniversary

of the Cuban Missile Crisis. In 1962, Bobby Kennedy, the brother of the president, went to Anatoly Dobrynin, the Soviet ambassador in Washington at the time, and they closed a deal on how to de-escalate the situation, and save the world from a nuclear war. Look at how different things are today. There is no Iranian embassy in Israel. There is no red line between the prime minister's office and the supreme leader. The world must stop Iran. This is not just an Israeli problem. The Iranian regime opposes every UN value: freedom, human rights, rule of law, women's rights — everything.

If you believe the international press and David Sanger's new book about covert campaigns, I am the only person in the world who has taken part in three counter-proliferation operations. Two were very successful, and spared the world from nuclear weapons in the hands of cruel, bloodthirsty dictators. The international community must take care of the third campaign, lest the barrel of a gun — and this time a nuclear gun — will look at all of us squarely in the face. Thank you.

RUDYARD GRIFFITHS: So there you see it on display: the discipline of an Israel Defense Forces officer who always completes his mission. Fareed Zakaria, you're up next.

FAREED ZAKARIA: Thank you so much. I really understand the position of the opposing team. I understand the fear, I understand the danger, and I understand the challenge. Let me put this in some historical perspective. Before the Cold War, the United States was the only country in the world with nuclear weapons. Then the Soviet Union acquired a nuclear weapon. And there were many people who felt — many highly influential people — that this was an absolute calamity, and that the only possible recourse for the United States was to engage in a pre-emptive war against the Soviet Union.

This was not a position held by wacky warmongers. Bertrand Russell, the pacifist philosopher, argued in favour of it. Harold Nicolson, the cool, unsentimental British diplomat, also argued in favour of it. But a man like Dwight Eisenhower understood that rollback, a strategy of pre-emptive war, would have huge costs and incur huge consequences. So he opted instead for a strategy called deterrence and containment: keep the Soviets in a box; put pressure on them so that they found it difficult to operate; and maintain the deterrent that says to them: If you try to do something, you will be annihilated.

Now remember, the Soviet Union at the time was regarded as a wild, crazy, revolutionary power bent on global revolution. Remember that Stalin had just sacrificed tens of millions of his people in World War II on the Eastern Front, something that was unfathomable to Western statesmen. The Soviets were routinely called "irrational," "crazy," "wild-eyed," and "messianic" — all of the things you have heard about the current Iranian regime. But we learned that the proper course of action was not rollback and pre-emptive war but containment and deterrence. And we saw this again in China. John Kennedy feared that if China went nuclear, twenty-five countries would go nuclear. Well, China did go nuclear.

And Mao was truly crazy: he openly talked about the need for nuclear war. He said it would require sacrifices but that it would be educational — half the world would be destroyed, but the other half would be socialists. Now that is a crazier, more messianic comment than anything the Iranian mullahs have ever said. Yet, what we learned was that Mao could be contained and deterred.

And, as Vali mentioned, we watched this in the country I grew up in, India. India and Pakistan used to fight a war every fifteen years. After independence, they fought three wars in thirty years. Then they got nuclear weapons. And in the last forty years, they haven't fought a war since. Now, you will, of course, see tensions and you will, of course, see crises like the Cuban Missile Crisis, because these powers are in conflict with one another. But what is extraordinary is that during the Cold War, despite this intense geopolitical rivalry, all of history would have suggested that the United States and the Soviet Union would have gone to war with one another. But they didn't, and that's because of nuclear weapons — because they were deterred, because of the fear of what it would mean. Margaret Thatcher understood this. In 1989 she gave a speech while standing beside Mikhail Gorbachev and said, "You and I, Mr. Secretary General, know that conventional weapons have never deterred war in Europe. But nuclear weapons have done so for forty years." She gave that speech in 1989, so that makes almost seventy years since the end of World War II.

When North Korea went nuclear, we were told that all of Asia was going to go nuclear — Japan would go nuclear, South Korea would go nuclear. You can understand why. South Korea is still in a state of active arms and at war with North Korea. And yet that hasn't happened. South Korea hasn't gone nuclear, Japan hasn't gone nuclear. The lesson of North Korea has been that if you're a third-rate dysfunctional country that manages to acquire a couple of crude nuclear devices, you remain a third-rate dysfunctional country with a couple of crude nuclear devices. Power does not flow from the barrels of a few rudimentary nuclear weapons. It flows from your GDP, from your innovation, from your technological prowess.

And so we come to Israel. And we come to the challenge that Iran places on that country. And what I would argue is that the Iranians, as Vali has pointed out, are cool, calculating, and shrewd, far more so in their rhetoric and certainly in their actions than any of the regimes we have talked about tonight. They will be deterred. They will be deterred by Israel's 200 to 500 nuclear weapons. They will also be deterred by Israel's second-strike capacity — its many submarines. And Iran will be deterred by America's vast arsenal of nuclear weapons.

And recall, Iran doesn't have any nuclear weapons yet. We are talking about a hypothetical situation. And yet what we are really talking about is a war in the Middle East where we go and strike a regime pre-emptively. And what would be the result? The Iranian regime would gain support at home. Every time foreigners have pre-emptively attacked a regime, it has had the effect of rallying the people around that regime. We would be able to destroy part of their infrastructure, but they would be able to rebuild it very quickly. Israel's own estimates are that they would delay the uranium enrichment program by two years. You would radicalize the Middle East and turn the mullahs and this regime into a much more popular force in the Middle East than it is now. Meanwhile, we have another option — a containment and deterrence strategy. We have enormous pressure on them. The sanctions have been crippling their economy. They have not been able to develop a nuclear weapon. The Israeli intelligence that I have received every year for the last ten years has suggested that Iran is one year away from getting a nuclear bomb. Either Israeli intelligence is very bad or we have been very good at deterring and containing Iran.

RUDYARD GRIFFITHS: Well, there's a professional broadcaster for you — one second to spare. Well done, Fareed. There's so much that we need to discuss, from proliferation to deterrence, but what I think is on the mind of many of the people in this room, gentlemen, is what's happened in the last few weeks between Israel and Gaza. Vali Nasr, let's start with you. You've argued that Iran is looking to acquire a nuclear device to dominate the Arab world, not to destroy Israel. Yet, as we've heard from General Yadlin, those very missiles — those very long-range missiles that were fired for the first time by Hamas and jihadists on Jerusalem and on Tel Aviv — were proudly provided by Iran. So, why is General Yadlin wrong about the intent of destruction, and why are you right about the impetus toward domination?

VALI NASR: First of all, Iran and Israel have been in low-level warfare with one another for a number of decades. You referred to the back and forth over what happened in south Lebanon with the bombing and then the retaliation that Iran launched in Argentina, and there have been attacks on Israel here and there. There have also been cyber attacks on Iran, some of their scientists have been assassinated, and they are striking back. However, launching nuclear weapons is a whole different order of magnitude in terms of escalation, particularly against a country that has several hundred nuclear warheads with a much more accurate ability to deliver them. And, as Fareed said, the Israelis have second-strike capabilities with their submarines. Iran is in no position to be able to take Israel on at that level.

Of course Iran would brandish these missiles very proudly. The regime wants to change the conversation in the Middle East from Syria and itself to the Arab-Israeli issue. Iranian leadership wants to tell the Arabs that they are providing ammunition to the Palestinians to stand up to Israel. In the past week it has gained a lot of ground in the Arab world because of these two things, because the limelight has shifted from them and what they are doing in Syria to the Arab–Israeli issue. It is seen as the only government in the region that is providing material support to the Palestinians. Again, it is cold calculation about what would promote their position in the region.

RUDYARD GRIFFITHS: Charles, it sounds rational. Cold, calculated, moving forward to shift attention away from what is happening in Syria. Why don't you buy that analysis?

CHARLES KRAUTHAMMER: This argument that Iran is acting purely from nationalistic motives — that it is merely cold and calculating — simply makes no sense in relation to Israel. Iran and Israel were allies, friends even, until the revolution. There is nothing intrinsic about Iranian national interest that drives the country to want to destroy Israel. It is precisely the ideology of the mullahs; it is precisely the theology of the mullahs; it is precisely the idea that the revolution in Iran was the harbinger, the beginning, the spark for the return of the Twelfth Imam, the restoration of the caliphate, and the return of Islam's place in the world — that's how the Ayatollah Khomeini explained it.

And in order to achieve that, they have been saying for the last year that the destruction of Israel is necessary as the starting point for the redemption of humanity. Is that nationalism speaking? Is that national interest speaking? Our opponents tonight are trying to pretend that somehow the Iranian regime is cold and calculating and nationalistic. If that is the case, why is it risking everything by supplying arms to Hezbollah and to Hamas? How does that promote Iranian national interest? How does Iran's involvement in the Syrian civil war promote their national interest? In Syria, there is growing hatred among Sunni Arabs toward the Iranian regime because

Iran is supplying arms to the Syrian government to help protect them — even sending the Revolutionary Guards into the country — to kill, imprison, and torture Sunni Muslims trying to achieve freedom there.

No, this is a highly ideologically driven regime, and at the top of its ideological and theological list is the annihilation of Israel. Our opponents are saying that it's rhetoric; that this is a nation that is only interested in its own national well-being. But it's plainly the opposite.

RUDYARD GRIFFITHS: Charles, let's have Fareed come back on this critical point of what the most recent conflict between Israel and Gaza indicates.

FAREED ZAKARIA: I have two points. Let me answer Charles's question first. The reason that the Iranians are espousing the Palestinian cause so vociferously is because this is a Shiite Persian regime that is trying to have dominance of the Middle East. How do you do that with a bunch of Arabs? By appropriating their most important cause.

If you go to the streets of Cairo, which I have done many times, what is striking when you visit shopkeepers is that they have a photograph of Mahmoud Ahmadinejad, a Shiite Persian, up in their shops. And if you ask them, why do you have that photograph? They say it's because he supports the Palestinians. The Iranian regime very cannily understands that by appropriating the core cause of the Arab street, they are, in effect, outwitting the Arab regimes themselves. They are saying to the Arab street, your governments are too scared of Washington to support the Palestinians fully, but we will support them. It gives them enormous street credibility. And by the way, it is what makes Arab countries very scared of publicly opposing Iran's rise to power.

As to your question about what the Gaza incursion tells us, it tells us one thing very clearly, particularly if you look at the reaction of Egypt and Turkey. There is now a new Middle East, and Israel is the superpower in that Middle East. We were told that the Egyptians under a new government were going to be different; they were Islamists, they were ideological — you know, Muslims are crazy and if you put one of them in power like that, you never know what is going to happen. But guess what Morsi did? He followed the Mubarak policy, which is basically to try and broker a deal between Hamas and Israel. And why did he do that? Because Israel's defense budget today is larger than that of all of its neighbours put together.

That doesn't even begin to get into the technological advantages Israel has; the qualitative advantages it has; the enormous advantage it has of being the only country in the Middle East with sophisticated nuclear weapons on sophisticated delivery systems. And so, once you confront these facts, it is clear that, yes, the Turks will make very fine speeches in favour of the Palestinians, and the Egyptians will shed crocodile tears, but none of them will do anything because — if I may say it in a word — they are deterred. Because if Israel did not believe in deterrence, why would it have gone through the enormous expense of building a nuclear arsenal? It is presumably to deter its enemies, not to use it.

RUDYARD GRIFFITHS: Amos, let's bring that direct point to you, because some people have commented that what the conflict between Israel and Gaza suggests is in fact that Israel needs some deterrence on its military action, on its range of military action, to force it to the bargaining table to find a solution through negotiation rather than conflict. How do you respond to that line of argument?

AMOS YADLIN: I don't know what we are doing in Gaza right now, because this debate is about Iran.

Basically, I believe the arguments that Cold War deterrence principles are going to work in the Middle East are wrong. Just listen to the Ayatollah Hashemi Rafsanjani. He is the former president of Iran, and used to describe Israel as a "one-bomb country," meaning very tiny, very small, and then would proudly proclaim that the Islamic nation could absorb three to four bombs. Is that deterrence? No, it is not.

When the Americans and the Soviets were doing deterrence calculations during the Cold War, both of these countries wanted to continue to exist on earth. When we deal with Iran, we are negotiating with people who think about the second world, the second life. They invented suicide bombing. They sent kids to open minefields during the war with Iraq. Yes, these people are rational, but it's not according to our definition of rational. It's different. And I am very, very worried about the way they are making their decisions.

RUDYARD GRIFFITHS: Let's spend one more moment on this before moving onto the question of proliferation, because that is a big one. Vali, you've written a series of books on Iran and it is the country in which you were born. Why is General Yadlin wrong to think that there is an irrational messianic force, maybe not among the Iranian people but among the elite and the leadership, who could make the decision of whether to engage in a nuclear conflict or not?

VALI NASR: The fact that people are willing to die for a cause is not unique to Muslims. During World War II, the Japanese used kamikaze pilots. Suicide bombings are the poor man's missile system; they have been proven to be very effective, and that's the reason they are still used. Secondly, rulers can always manipulate the popular beliefs of foot soldiers to get them to sacrifice themselves for a greater cause. It has happened all over the world. You see it in many Muslim countries, not only in Iran: the person, the foot soldier willing to commit suicide for a cause, who can believe in anything, but the generals don't believe in that line of thinking.

The Iranian leaders are old men. They didn't get to that age by actually believing in suicide bombing; not one of them carried out suicide bombings against the Shah's regime; not one of them has sent his own sons to carry out suicide missions. Yes, of course, General Yadlin is right in that the morality and ethics of this regime are abhorrent and they use poor, uneducated, fanatical kids to achieve their strategic objectives. But there is no evidence that Iranian rulers actually make their calculations on the basis of wishing to expedite their own departure to the next world.

RUDYARD GRIFFITHS: Let's move on to the theme of nuclear proliferation because it is a key one. Over the last week or so, we've caught up with a few international policy thinkers to get their reflections on this debate, and we are going to bring them to you in the form of video clips now. The first is Sen. George Mitchell, whom we spoke to in Washington, D.C., earlier this week. He is the former U.S. senate majority leader but, more importantly, he was Barack Obama's U.S. special envoy for Middle East peace until 2011. Let's listen to that clip, and then I am going to have Charles react.

GEORGE MITCHELL: Thank you, Rudyard, and good evening. The debate on this subject has tended to focus on the threat to Israel from a nuclear-armed Iran: that is a serious concern, which I share, and I am sure it will be discussed this evening. There is another aspect of this subject that I think deserves discussion as well and that is the threat to the nuclear non-proliferation regime or, stated more simply, the danger of the rapid spread of nuclear weapons to many countries.

The United States led the world into the nuclear age, and ever since has also led the effort to restrain the spread of these highly destructive weapons — with some success. In the half-century since the first atomic bomb was exploded over the desert in New Mexico, nine countries have come to possess nuclear weapons. But the number of countries with the capability to possess these weapons is many more than nine. Those countries, which have voluntarily refrained from developing nuclear weapons, one of which, of course, is Canada, have relied instead on the NPT and on American leadership.

If Iran gets a nuclear weapon, that could change. It could trigger an arms race in the Middle East as several countries there move quickly to get a weapon. And it is already a highly volatile and very dangerous place. Right now, Israelis and Palestinians are dying. The ancient hostility between Persians and Arabs remains high, as does the internal conflict between Sunni and Shia Muslims, which has gone on since the founding of Islam.

RUDYARD GRIFFITHS: Charles, it was a big part of your opening argument, the case for stopping Iran in order to allow the non-proliferation treaty to continue. Go deeper on that for us. Why do you think this particular region is so different from the examples that Fareed and Vali have given with China, with Russia, with India and Pakistan, and, most recently, with North Korea?

CHARLES KRAUTHAMMER: Because the conditions — the geopolitical conditions — are radically different. Our opponents tonight keep referring back to this stable, Cold War deterrence between two established world powers, the U.S. and the Soviet Union. But, first of all, the nostalgia is slightly overdone. Anybody who lived through October 1962 knows how close we came — within hours — to a nuclear war between the United States and the Soviet Union. So even this one great example of how we can live with this indefinitely shows how inherently unstable it is — and Kissinger spoke about that. However, it was the only alternative. Once the Soviets and the U.S had 10,000 weapons, there was no other option. But we're now at a point in history where Iran has no nuclear weapons. And we can avoid that. We can avoid a Cuban Missile Crisis.

Why would we choose a world in which Iran, this unstable, extremist Islamist, aggressive power, would possess these weapons — a country that declares its intention to annihilate a UN member state? And you will have noticed that our opponents tonight have said nothing about the issue of hyper-proliferation. They keep referring to this single example of stable, bilateral deterrence. But what will happen in the Middle East, as everybody understands, is that you will get all these countries — small, but some of them rich, some technologically advanced — developing nukes. And then you will have a situation where you go from nuclear checkers, which is relatively easy — America and Soviets — to three-dimensional chess. That is the difference between the Cold War example and the current issue of a nuclear-armed Iran.

What would result today in the region is a nuclearized Middle East, with shifting alliances, revolutionary governments, and unstable regimes. Imagine nuclear weapons in the hands of seven or eight of these countries, countries where they could easily have accidental or unauthorized use. They don't have a tradition of civilian control of nuclear weapons as in the West. It would be so easy to turn one officer or another, as we have seen in Afghanistan. Every day, an Afghan officer will turn on a Western ally. And there is also the issue of regime —

RUDYARD GRIFFITHS: I'm getting signals from people who want in on this, so I'm going to go quickly to Fareed, to Amos, and then to Vali.

FAREED ZAKARIA: It turns out we have an actual historical experiment as to whether or not proliferation would occur in the Middle East. It turns out there used to be a Middle East that had no nuclear weapons, and then one Middle Eastern power introduced nuclear weapons into the region. The name of that country is, of course, Israel. Israel now has between 200 and 500 very sophisticated weapons, depending on whom you believe. As it turns out, none of the countries surrounding Israel, which are technically still at war with Israel, have gone nuclear as a result.

So if the hyper-proliferation scenario that Charles is so devoted to were true, why is it that, when their sworn enemy — the country that the opposing team keeps reminding us the Arabs hate and want to get rid of — got nuclear weapons, it did not trigger proliferation?

CHARLES KRAUTHAMMER: Let me answer that.

FAREED ZAKARIA: The truth is that every country that has received some kind of security guarantee from the United States has chosen not to proliferate. That is true of Japan; that is true of South Korea; that is true of Canada. Charles Krauthammer's touching faith in the NPT is rich. The truth of the matter is that the reason that people are not proliferating is that they get guarantees from the United States, guarantees that the United States has provided to the moderate Arab states and, of course, has provided to Israel. But you ask —

RUDYARD GRIFFITHS: A quick rebuttal —

CHARLES KRAUTHAMMER: You asked a question. Is it rhetorical or were you asking a real question? You asked: Why is it that when Israel acquires a nuclear weapon, you don't get hyper-proliferation? The answer is easy and simple. Israel has no intention of annihilating any neighbouring countries. Do you think Egypt, Saudi Arabia, and others live in terror that one day, out of the blue, Israel is going to destroy Cairo or Riyadh? No. The reason that the Israeli weapon is not a threat and that it doesn't cause fear is because everybody in the region understands that Israel is not going to start a nuclear war; it is simply inconceivable, whereas Iran, which is intervening in Gaza, arming Hezbollah, intervening in Syria and elsewhere, is a nation that, when it threatens to annihilate another country, people take it seriously. And the Saudis aren't acting or being cynical when they say that if Iran gets a nuclear weapon —

RUDYARD GRIFFITHS: Wait a second, Charles, equal time for all of the debaters. I'm going to go to Vali and then back to Amos.

VALI NASR: First of all, as you've already said, threat is in the eyes of the beholder and the Arab countries do take Israel's nuclear capabilities as a strategic game-changer — maybe not for fear of annihilation, but it is certainly a strategic game-changer. However, there is no evidence that hyper-proliferation would actually happen if Iran possessed a nuclear weapon. It seems to be more of an American argument in order to make the case against Iran going nuclear.

In fact, it looks like we have done more to goad countries to say that they want to go nuclear. We are supporting Egypt, the UAE, Saudi Arabia, Jordan, all of them, to actually establish nuclear facilities. And I don't think countries can easily build nuclear capabilities in the Middle East. Iran's nuclear program goes back several decades to the time of the Shah. Most of these countries we are talking about don't have the infrastructure to build a nuclear weapons program and, as General Yadlin already stated, Saudi Arabia can go to Pakistan to get a weapon if they so choose. If that's the case, then what are we doing here? These two countries are our allies. The UAE is our ally. We have much more leverage to prevent proliferation in this region now than we had with Iraq. It seems to me we are making the case for all of these countries to go nuclear because it proves our case against Iran, but there is no real evidence for it.

RUDYARD GRIFFITHS: General Yadlin?

AMOS YADLIN: The fact that you tell a lie and repeat it again and again does not make it true. I am speaking about the number of bombs in Israel's possession. Israel declares that it will not be the first to introduce nuclear weapons to the Middle East. Israel will not be the first to use them in a conflict. It is the only country in the Middle East that is under threat that it will be wiped off the map. This is historically true. So, I believe Israel has behaved very responsibly. As Fareed has said, we have had four wars with Egypt and never considered using anything other than conventional weapons. So it's different behaviour if you compare it to the way the Iranians are acting and speaking. I am describing what they are doing all over the Middle East, and you cannot ignore or deny it.

Vali, you and I both read the WikiLeaks. The Saudis are saying that they are not going to tolerate a nuclear Iran. And believe me, they are your allies — allies of the United States — but they don't trust you anymore. They don't trust you because of what happened in Egypt; they don't trust you because you are not stopping Iran from becoming nuclear; they don't trust you because of the Israeli–Palestinian issue. And the Saudis will become nuclear, no doubt about it.

We've already spoken about a multi-player balance in the Middle East, which is so unstable and so dangerous. It is not only us who don't want to live in a region like this. *You* also don't want to live in a multiple-player nuclear Middle East because if Iran becomes the hegemon, the price of oil will be $200 or $300 a barrel and it will stay there forever. So it is your problem and not only ours.

RUDYARD GRIFFITHS: Two final interventions on this point. We're going to go to Fareed, and then Charles, you'll have the last word. Then we'll move on to another topic.

FAREED ZAKARIA: I think it is very important for us to have a conversation about what happens if the strategy that the opposing team wants takes place. We are living in a world of bad choices. That's the world of international relations; that is the world of international politics. You don't have wonderful, clean solutions to make the problems go away. So, imagine the scenario: the United States or Israel engages in the third Middle Eastern war in a decade. We go and strike Iran. What is going to happen?

AMOS YADLIN: We haven't suggested it, by the way.

FAREED ZAKARIA: If we cannot tolerate a nuclear Iran, the logical consequence is one you will have to live with, so let's play it out. What will happen is that the regime will get strengthened. It happens everywhere. One week after 9/11, George Bush's approval ratings were 91 percent. Another consequence is that the Green Movement will be destroyed in Iran. The regime will be able to rebuild its capabilities very easily. The nuclear budget for Iran — for the nuclear civilian program — is currently $300 million. They make about $50 billion off their oil revenues. This is a drop in the bucket for them. They will have radicalized the Middle East. They will have gained purchase on the Arab street.

All of this for a two-, maybe three-year delay? Then what are you going to do? Bomb them every two years? Hope that one day, that somehow in our fantasy version, the country that we keep bombing turns into a moderate, liberal democracy and suddenly embraces Western values? What is far more likely to happen, of course, is that they will become even more radicalized.

Imagine if we had done what Charles wanted in the 1950s and had a rollback strategy. He says we couldn't have done it with the Soviet Union because they had 10,000 missiles. But they didn't pursue this strategy in the 1950s, and there were many people arguing that we should have engaged in a pre-emptive war. Imagine what would have happened then. Imagine if we had engaged in a pre-emptive war with China — would any of these regimes have mellowed? Would they have integrated into the world the way they have? No, they would have been radicalized, violent, unstable regimes, and that is the fate we are condemning ourselves to if we launch another war in the Middle East.

RUDYARD GRIFFITHS: Well, Charles —

CHARLES KRAUTHAMMER: I'd like to answer. If we're going to ask questions in here, we should at least accept that there might be answers to them. Fareed is giving us this scenario about what will happen if and when Israel or the United States attacks Iran's nuclear facilities. He says people will rally to the government and the Green Movement will be destroyed. And he went on and on, and elaborated with all these imaginary details.

The problem with his analysis is that we have two actual empirical, historical examples of exactly what he is talking about — the pre-emptive de-nuclearization of a country. General Yadlin, sitting here beside me, was involved in the first — he dropped the bombs on Iraq's nuclear site in 1981. And what was the reaction from Iraq? Zero.

FAREED ZAKARIA: They rebuilt their nuclear program, however.

AMOS YADLIN: It took much longer than two years.

CHARLES KRAUTHAMMER: Did they attack? Did they go to war and rally? No. That is my number one point.

FAREED ZAKARIA: They rebuilt their nuclear program, though — precisely what I pointed out. During the Gulf War, inspectors found an Iraqi nuclear program, which had been built after Osirak —

AMOS YADLIN: It took ten years, not two years.

CHARLES KRAUTHAMMER: That was ten years later. The West gained a decade, not just two years, because when they went into Iraq, they found that it had not rebuilt and created a bomb. Number two example: in 2007 there was an attack on a Syrian nuclear facility that the government had built with the help of the North Koreans. Reaction? Zero. Syria didn't even announce the attack. Second, imagine if we had not done that? If the Israelis — acting on behalf of the West — had not done that? What would be happening in Syria today?

The world is terrified about the loose chemical and biological weapons that are in Syria — that the regime has declared are there. Al Qaeda and jihadist groups in Syria could easily acquire them. That is why the U.S. is so vigilant, standing on the border with Jordan, ready to pre-empt the transfer of these weapons. It is this pre-emption that ensures that no terrorist organizations get their hands on nukes. The consideration of hyper-proliferation is vastly important, and it is absurd to think that somehow there would be this great reaction of rallying to the regime as a result of pre-emptive action.

The Iranian regime's suppression of the Green Revolution revealed just how much the majority of people, particularly the young, hate the regime. If there were, for example, a U.S. strike that not only hit the nukes but attacked elements of regime strength like the Revolutionary Guards, it could be an occasion for a revival of the Green Revolution. Remember, the Revolutionary Guards who torture young people on the streets are not heroes, and they would not become heroes were they to be the victims of a U.S. or Israeli attack on nuclear facilities. I believe an attack could have the opposite effect — galvanizing a population that hates an oppressive, theological regime at a time when the regime would be at its weakest.

RUDYARD GRIFFITHS: Vali, you're the expert on Iran. Tell us why that is not true.

VALI NASR: To respond to your first point, Syria and Iraq are not Iran. In terms of physical size, capability, location, size of population, the amount of weight they have in the Middle East, they are different. The reaction from Iran could potentially be the opposite. Secondly, I don't know of any population that is going to side with the outsiders bombing their country, especially because this is not about democracy. We are not putting sanctions on Iran because of democracy and human rights and we would not bomb them in the future because of democracy and human rights. We would bomb them and pressure them for something that the Iranian people potentially believe in — the nuclear program. It's their technology, and their government has told them that this is for peaceful purposes. The Iranians are probably as affectionate about their nuclear program as the Pakistanis and Indians are about theirs.

CHARLES KRAUTHAMMER: What about Libya last year? We bombed and the population applauded us.

VALI NASR: When you bombed them, you were not

bombing them for their nuclear program, you were bombing them to protect them from an authoritarian regime.

CHARLES KRAUTHAMMER: You just said you know of no case when a government is attacked and its people rally on behalf of the attacker. I just gave you an example that happened within the past two years.

VALI NASR: No, the pretext matters. What makes you think that Iranians would rally behind us? Because of when we intervened in Iran in 1953 and the reaction we got suggests the Iranians would side with us now? Or the example of the Iran-Iraq war when as soon as Saddam attacked, even the moderate liberal democratic population —

CHARLES KRAUTHAMMER: Because they hate a regime that shoots young women in the street, tortures demonstrators, and then delivers the body to the family. That is why they would rally, because —

FAREED ZAKARIA: Charles, did you get the last letter mixed up? Because we heard all of this about the Iraq war: the Iraqis were going to love us because we were bombing them into freedom and democracy and —

RUDYARD GRIFFITHS: Gentlemen, I just want to give our guest, who has come all the way from Israel to be here, some time on the stage.

AMOS YADLIN: I'd like to remind the audience of the resolution today. The resolution is not whether to attack Iran or not. The resolution is whether the world can live with a nuclear Iran. And since our opponents don't have arguments, they moved to the topic of a possible attack. We are not suggesting that we should attack Iran. We suggest not letting Iran become nuclear by having tough sanctions, by doing everything short of war, and this has not been done yet.

Only in the last year has the world imposed crippling sanctions. If we had done it a decade ago, we would not be debating this issue right now. This is a hated regime and I have often heard the argument that if you just sanction the country, the people will rally behind the regime, but that has never happened. There are only a small number of old Iranians. Sixty-five percent of them are very young and never knew the Shah; they blame the Islamic Republic for the bad conditions in Iran. And I think that by imposing tougher sanctions, we will buy enough time to change the regime. We do not think we should attack Iran unless it is the last resort.

To reiterate, I am not speaking about invading another country. What you did in Iraq was a mistake. But it is important to remember that the U.S. has a very good air force that could surgically solve the problem in Iran in the future, but I am not recommending it yet.

RUDYARD GRIFFITHS: Let's move on to another topic. You know, what is a Munk Debate without a little bit of a contribution from Dr. Henry Kissinger? We caught up with Dr. Kissinger in New York last week. Let's have a listen to his intervention in this debate.

HENRY KISSINGER: Thank you, Rudyard. For a decade and a half, American presidents from both political parties have declared that an Iranian nuclear military capability is unacceptable, and that no option is off the table in preventing it. If Iran emerges from this process with military nuclear capability, the psychological and strategic balance in the region will be transformed. The countries of the region and elsewhere will look to the development of nuclear weapons for their own security, and non-proliferation as an international goal will be over or seriously jeopardized. The credibility of Western strategy will also be severely damaged. It is essential that the United States and its allies define what they mean by "Iranian nuclear military capability" and what they mean by the term "unacceptable."

RUDYARD GRIFFITHS: Fareed, let me start with you. I want to zero in on a key line of what Dr. Kissinger said: "The credibility of Western strategy will be severely damaged." Your president, in the context of this recent election, had to walk toward a red line on Iran that is very close to our resolution tonight. We are talking about capability — it's about the ability to assemble a device as opposed to having a working device. So, in some ways, has the train already left the station? Is the U.S. position able to walk back from what Dr. Krauthammer and General Yadlin are arguing?

FAREED ZAKARIA: First of all, how do you argue with that accent? Dr. Kissinger was my partner the last time I participated in a Munk Debate, so I naturally have great respect for him.

I think that the United States' position on this issue, which is a somewhat technical point but worth going into, is understandably ambiguous. You do not want to signal in advance at exactly what point you would go to war. Do you know who else has exactly the same position? The government of Israel. Even though the Israeli prime minister has been asking Washington to draw a red line, Israel itself has not drawn a red line, and I would argue they are right not to draw a red line. You want to keep the other side guessing. You want to keep the pressure on. You don't want to be entirely clear as to when you would take action. You don't want to give the other person your timetable for war.

It's one thing if they do something — like invading a country — that triggers an obvious response. But in a situation like this, we retain much more room to manoeuvre and much more flexibility if we maintain some degree of strategic ambiguity, as the Israelis are doing. It is important to point out that the Iranians do not have nuclear weapons. In fact, there is something worth pointing out here — not only do they not have nuclear weapons, but the Supreme Leader of Iran has issued a fatwa, a religious edict, saying that it would be un-Islamic for the country to possess them, and that the founder of the regime, the Ayatollah Khomeini, also believed this.

Now, of course they could be lying. But it would be rather odd for a regime that relies on fatwas for its legitimacy to unnecessarily issue these edicts. Nobody is asking them to say this stuff, right? Therefore, the fact that they are doing so may also suggest that Iran may have a complicated calculation of its own; that they want some kind of capacity that will buy them a certain degree of influence, but they are not seeking to have an arsenal of nuclear weapons all ready to go. That reality is the one we have to live with when trying to figure out exactly what Iranian action would trigger an American or Israeli response. And that's why the Americans and the Israelis are, understandably, maintaining that ambiguity.

CHARLES KRAUTHAMMER: Can I comment on that? "Of course he could be lying." That is an interesting understatement. Here is a regime that, as Fareed has argued, has allowed its currency to depreciate by 60 percent, has had its economy completely wrecked, and has been isolated because it is pursuing a nuclear program. And you are asking us to believe that the Ayatollah's saying, "Oh we aren't really interested," ought to supersede what we are seeing in front of our own eyes?

FAREED ZAKARIA: Saddam Hussein did all of those things and he didn't have a nuclear weapon, it turned out —

CHARLES KRAUTHAMMER: Do you think Iran is faking a nuclear program? Do you think the facility outside of Qom is a theatrical set?

FAREED ZAKARIA: I'm pointing out that Saddam Hussein —

CHARLES KRAUTHAMMER: I'm talking about the real world and what is happening right now.

FAREED ZAKARIA: Saddam Hussein was in the real world, not in a fantasy. I don't know if you got that.

CHARLES KRAUTHAMMER: Saddam Hussein didn't have a nuclear weapon. And you're saying that therefore Iran is faking it, too? Iran is faking its nuclear program?

FAREED ZAKARIA: No, it has an active nuclear civilian program.

CHARLES KRAUTHAMMER: Civilian?

FAREED ZAKARIA: You want an answer? I believe that serious Iranian scholars and intelligence analysts are unsure about whether the country has decided to weaponize completely or to stop just short because that gets them most of the benefits and the influence that they seek without actually incurring the costs. That is an issue, for example, on which American and Israeli intelligence and the former head of Mossad would agree with me —

RUDYARD GRIFFITHS: It's great that you brought that up because that is an absolutely key point, and I want Amos Yadlin to respond to that. It's about walking up to that line and not going over it.

AMOS YADLIN: I think somebody has to understand the Iranian strategy. As Vali Nasr knows very well, the Iranians are smart, sophisticated —

FAREED ZAKARIA: But crazy.

AMOS YADLIN: . . . and they have learned from history. And history told them that Libya, Syria, and Iraq did it wrong, but that Pakistan, India, and North Korea did it right. And they have learned a lesson. They are not going to make a bomb as fast as possible. They are going to build a bomb in as safe a way as possible.

And we have discovered they are using a sophisticated strategy. Iran wants to develop a nuclear program that Zakaria and others will call civilian, but it is not civilian: it is very unnecessary, wide, and covert. They have developed all the capabilities that will enable them to become nuclear at the time of their choosing. Strategically, they have decided to assemble a nuclear weapon. Otherwise they would not suffer all the sanctions and all the difficulties that they are going through now. They would not do that just for a civilian program. They want to go nuclear when it is convenient for them. And it will be very difficult to stop them at that time. The regime is smart. Remember that the Iranian nuclear weapons issue was referred to the UN Security Council — not by Israel, not by the Zionist movement — but by the UN watchdog in Vienna, the International Atomic Energy Agency (IAEA), because they cheat, because they conceal, because they lie —

FAREED ZAKARIA: On which we agree.

AMOS YADLIN: . . . because the IAEA found a high level of enrichment, because Iran didn't let the IAEA interview their scientists and their heads of programs, and they didn't let any intelligence officers know exactly where things were going. Strategically, the weapons are there. They only have one mile left to build, and that is what they intend to do if we let them continue with the program.

RUDYARD GRIFFITHS: I want to be conscious of our time, and we need to get to closing statements so that we can have a final, second audience vote within our timeline. So, Vali Nasr, I want to give you the last word here before we move on to our closing statements.

VALI NASR: There are many strategic reasons why Iran would want nuclear capability, a virtual nuclear program, or an actual bomb. As I said, it has to do with regime survival and national interests. But if what you are saying is true, then sanctions and diplomacy will not work and we are back to our previous argument. Do we want to go to war to stop Iran or are we going to agree that we can handle this through containment and deterrence?

You said that aggressive sanctions and international pressure may work and that maybe diplomacy in the second term will work. But according to you, they have already made the decision that they are going to build up their nuclear capabilities because it comes down to the fact that they don't want to have the fate of Syria, Iraq, and Libya, and they want to feel the same sense of security as North Korea and Pakistan. And if that is the case, then the only option on the table is that we either contain and deter them or we go to war with them.

RUDYARD GRIFFITHS: We're now going to bring the podium out so that closing statements can take place. We're going to do the closing statements in the opposite order of the opening statements. So, Fareed Zakaria, that means that you are up first.

FAREED ZAKARIA: When I was a kid in college, I invited Caspar Weinberger, [Ronald] Reagan's defense secretary, to campus to speak. There was a huge amount of commotion and many protests against him, all from the left. There were many people, from an audience of this size, that started standing up and chanting against him. And they kept saying, "Deterrence is a lie," because in those days it was the left that didn't understand deterrence, because they were emotional and irrational, and they felt that there surely must be another option. And it was the wise heads, the sane people on the right, steeped in realism and history and tragedy, who reminded us of the need for deterrence. One such person put it very brilliantly when he said, "Almost once every twenty-five years, a new generation discovers the horrors of the bomb and the paradoxes of deterrence and looks for a way out. But alas," he said, "there is no way out. Deterrence, like old age, is intolerable, until one considers the alternative." That was Charles Krauthammer, about twenty-five years ago.

So what I want to say to Charles is, "Come home, Charles Krauthammer." Come home to the sad, necessary task of building a powerful containment and deterrence strategy against Iran. Of course, nobody wants an Iran with nuclear weapons. Of course, we all want to place every obstacle in their way and to put as much pressure on them as possible to desist. And of course, we want to have precisely the same strategy we had in the Cold War, of detaining and deterring them, so that eventually we create circumstances where the young people of Iran can take their country back; these young people who will have acquired a desire for modernity and for integration with the West, and for freedom and liberty. And that is the course we are trying to move on. But there is no fantasy solution out there. How do we decide that we cannot tolerate this and we will go to war instead? That we are going to pre-emptively strike another country in the Middle East, and assume they will love us and embrace us for it? And then hope that all of the problems of the Middle East will go away because we got rid of that evil thing — deterrence.

Alas, that isn't how it works. International politics will persist, international rivalries will persevere, and the Middle East will continue to be a complicated place. Haven't we just gone through a decade of two wars in the Middle East, both of which were sold to us on the promise that this was going to usher in a new era in which everyone was going to love the United States and the West, and all the problems that existed would be gone? And yet we find ourselves in the same situation.

So I say, come home, Charles Krauthammer, come home to the kind of reason and history and logic that you once so powerfully believed in and promoted. Don't give in just because these guys are different, because they're brown. Don't believe that because of these reasons, we have to have fantastic solutions.

RUDYARD GRIFFITHS: Oh, Google! The things it allows us to find out about each other! Up next, Amos Yadlin.

AMOS YADLIN: Once again, I have to remind you that this debate is not about attacking Iran. This debate is about not letting Iran become nuclear, because we cannot afford to live in a world with a nuclear Iran. This is not the same story as the Cold War. This is a regime calling for the destruction of another country. I do not remember either the United States or the Soviet Union wanting to destroy each other on principle. So today is another story, and I think people underestimate what will happen to the NPT if Iran becomes nuclear, and they underestimate what kind of world we will live in if Iran becomes nuclear.

It is not about the issue of deterrence vis-à-vis Iran. It is about the issue of proliferation all over the Middle East. I am a general — I have fought in many wars. Nobody hates wars more than me. I have been there. I saw the blood; I saw the pain; I saw the waste of life; I saw the waste of resources. I heard the cries of widows and the orphans. We don't call for wars. We call for the world to wake up and stop Iran before there is a nuclear war.

And when you run out of arguments, as our opponents did, you speak about the war that nobody supports. We advocate for the isolation of Iran and the implementation of a very tough sanctions regime against the country. And we want the whole world to join, not only the West. We need the Russians, the Chinese, the Indians — because Iran must be stopped. Iran is not North Korea. North Korea is not threatening the whole of East Asia, nor does it want to become the hegemon. Iran wants to become the hegemon of the Middle East. And what will happen if Iran becomes the dominant power in the Middle East today is very similar to what happened in Europe in the 1940s. And remember, we cannot allow that again.

As an intelligence officer you have to answer two questions: What are the enemy's capabilities and what are the enemy's intentions? With capabilities, if you have good sources, you have good answers. How many missiles are in their possession? How many centrifuges are spinning? How many kilograms of enriched uranium do they have? With intentions, you have to be much more cautious. But the Iranians openly tell everybody their intentions: they want to destroy Israel. We have to take it very seriously and stop Iran from becoming nuclear. Thank you.

RUDYARD GRIFFITHS: Dean Nasr, you're next.

VALI NASR: I take General Yadlin's cautions and warnings quite seriously, and I do think that there are important and stark choices that face us right now and will face the new American administration going forward. We think the biggest issue in the Middle East right now is Iran, because it is a dictatorial regime that is abusing its population; because it is taunting Israel and its neighbours; because the regime is supporting terrorism; and because it is now going nuclear to boot. But when we think about decisions regarding Iran, we also have to remember that every decision has a context. The context is the following: Iran is not the only issue in the region. We are also seeing a Middle East that is falling apart all across the board: from Tunisia to Libya to Egypt to Bahrain, regime after regime is becoming unstable. We are seeing a rise in extremism. We are seeing a major shift in this region. We are not going to be dealing with Iran in a vacuum, and therefore the decisions we make have to be made with a view to what it means for the region.

We are also facing a United States that is tired of war; the country led two big wars in the Middle East recently and doesn't have a record to show for its efforts. It has spent trillions of dollars — a lot of blood and treasure — and it has not been able to accomplish its objectives in Afghanistan or in Iraq. And it is very clear that these days the Americans are more interested in nation-building at home, as the president put it, than transforming the Middle East. This is an important context to bear in mind.

Now, hopefully, the Iranian regime will change

as Dr. Krauthammer and General Yadlin have said. Hopefully, the administration will take diplomacy very seriously and by some miracle there is a breakthrough in the short run, or that sanctions really change the Iranian government's mind and they change course. But the clocks for diplomacy, for sanctions, for regime change in Iran are not synchronized with the clock for building Iran's nuclear capability. It is quite likely — and quite possible — that Iran may go nuclear before any of these things take effect; before sanctions, as rigorous as they are, produce a result; or before there is a successful democracy movement. If that is the case, we are really left with two choices: we either find a way to contain and deter a nuclear Iran or we have another war in the Middle East.

And if we go to war with Iran, then we have to be prepared for what that war would entail. And it could very well be that it would be far more costly and far more destabilizing to the region than the wars in Iraq and Afghanistan. We started sectarian war in the Middle East. Commentators have lamented that we started the Shia–Sunni war. Another war would be equally intolerable. Thank you.

RUDYARD GRIFFITHS: Charles Krauthammer, you have three minutes on the clock and the final word.

CHARLES KRAUTHAMMER: So much error, so little time. But I will address two points. Yes, I believe in every word I wrote in defense of deterrence in 1984 when dealing with the U.S. and the Soviet Union. And it remains true today. But the idea that some technique like deterrence, because it worked in one context, will therefore always work, is mindless.

I would say to my friend Fareed, "Wake up." Wake up to the reality that Israel–Iran is not the U.S.–Soviet Union. Wake up to the fact that the nature of the regime is completely different; that the regime in Iran, unlike the atheistic regime in the Soviet Union, has an apocalyptic, millennialist idea of history and sees itself as the instrument of that idea. Wake up to the idea that in the seventy years of the existence of the Soviet Union they never once sent out a suicide bomber, but that in Iran, martyrdom is the royal road to heaven. Wake up to the idea that the jihadists we are fighting around the world live by the words of al Qaeda, "You love life, we love death." Try deterring that. Wake up to the fact that the nature of the Cold War dispute was completely different. Russia was engaged in an ideological contest with the United States; it never sought to wipe it off the map. Iran believes that the existence of Israel is a crime against humanity and an illness that it has to cure.

And lastly, wake up to the fact that the Iranians themselves, the mullahs, have told us what they intend to achieve in a nuclear exchange with Israel. President Rafsanjani has said that dropping an atomic bomb on Israel would leave nothing there, but the same event in the Muslim world would just produce "damages." In other words, Israel would forever and instantly be wiped off the map, whereas the *umma*, the Muslim nation of

1.8 billion people, would be damaged but would endure. There is a radical difference in history between deterrence in the '80s and deterrence today. To mindlessly apply it and say that it worked in the past, so it will work in the future is completely unwarranted.

And remember the stakes — we are assured by our opponents tonight that deterrence will work. They don't know, and we don't know, if deterrence definitely will work, but imagine the risks if they are wrong. Six millions Jews will be dead, Israel will be eradicated, there will be hyper-proliferation in the Middle East, and Iran will dominate the Middle East and the oil economy of the world. Do any of you want to live with that? Thank you very much.

RUDYARD GRIFFITHS: Well, ladies and gentlemen, it is clear why people have called this debate one of the toughest global foreign policy challenges of a generation. We've had two sharply contrasting arguments tonight, eloquently presented by two teams of debaters, so a big round of applause for all of our speakers. Well done.

Let me reiterate something Peter Munk has said at these debates in the past. It is one thing to give a set-piece speech on a subject you are intimately familiar with; it is another thing to come before an informed audience like this and to make your case with passion and conviction. Now, the question before all of us is, which of these two teams of debaters has been able to sway public opinion in this hall?

I'm glad I don't have a ballot because I think it is

going to be a tough vote. But before we have that second vote, let us just quickly remember how people voted at the commencement of tonight's debate: 60 percent supported the resolution, 24 percent were against it and 16 percent were undecided, and a large number of you were open to changing your vote. We will announce the results in the south lobby. Thanks again, everyone, for coming. It was a great debate.

Summary: The pre-debate vote was 60 percent in favour of the resolution; 24 percent against; and 22 percent of voters were undecided. The final vote showed a disappearance of the undecided voters, with 58 percent in favour of the motion and 42 percent against it. Given the shift in votes, the victory goes to the team arguing against the resolution, Vali Nasr and Fareed Zakaria.

CHARLES KRAUTHAMMER IN CONVERSATION WITH HANNAH SUNG

HANNAH SUNG: For this particular Munk Debate the question is about Iran and nuclear capabilities. You were saying that the world cannot and should not tolerate a nuclear-powered Iran. Why?

CHARLES KRAUTHAMMER: You have to look at it from three perspectives. From the global perspective, if Iran — the greatest exporter of terror in the world — gets nuclear weapons, the idea of non-proliferation, preventing it from going to other countries, is dead. The entire Gulf region, all of the Arab states, are going to go nuclear. Saudi Arabia, Egypt, a non-Arab Turkey, Syria — can you imagine Syria with nuclear weapons? We don't even know who's going to be in charge of Syria. That's what the world will be like the morning after Iran goes nuclear.

Second, we need to look at it from a regional perspective. If Iran goes nuclear, it becomes the dominant power in the Middle East. It controls world oil; it controls and dominates the Arab world. Once they have nukes, any state that doesn't have nukes is going to be a client and supplicate to Iran. It will be in control of the world economy. Imagine what would have happened if Saddam Hussein had not been disarmed by Israel, which attacked Iraq's nuclear reactor ten years earlier? Imagine if Saddam had possessed nuclear weapons when he invaded Kuwait? He'd still be in charge of Kuwait, and be in control of the world oil in the Middle East.

The last of my three reasons has to do with Israel. Iran is dedicated to the utter eradication and annihilation of Israel, and all it needs is a half-dozen bombs and it can do to the Jewish people in Israel what Hitler needed six years to do — to kill six million of them. There are six million Jews in Israel. It would take an afternoon to do it, with half a dozen bombs.

VALI NASR IN CONVERSATION WITH HANNAH SUNG

HANNAH SUNG: Vali Nasr, very nice to meet you. This Munk Debate is on the question of a nuclear-powered Iran. You were saying that, yes, we can tolerate a nuclear Iran. Can you explain why?

VALI NASR: We would not like to see Iran go nuclear, but if it does go nuclear, it is not the end of the world for us. We've dealt with difficult countries, ideological countries, aggressive countries, that have gained nuclear weapons — from the Soviet Union, to communist China, to North Korea, to Pakistan — and every time containment and deterrence has worked. And the argument that somehow Iran is a breed apart, that its leadership is irrational, that it doesn't respond to the logic of containment and deterrence, is not supported by fact.

The Iranian regime has been there for thirty years. Yes, it does do things that disrupt the flow of international affairs that we don't like, but nevertheless we can see that its goals and aims are very much the ones that we are quite familiar with — national interest, survival, and projection of power — and we can deal with those things. So, we would not like to see Iran go nuclear, but if they do, we can tolerate it.

ACKNOWLEDGEMENTS

The Munk Debates are the product of the public-spiritedness of a remarkable group of civic-minded organizations and individuals. First and foremost, these debates would not be possible without the vision and leadership of the Aurea Foundation. Founded in 2006 by Peter and Melanie Munk, the Aurea Foundation supports Canadian individuals and institutions involved in the study and development of public policy. The debates are the foundation's signature initiative, a model for the kind of substantive public policy conversation Canadians can foster globally. Since their creation in 2008, the foundation has underwritten the entire cost of each semi-annual debate. The debates have also benefited from the input and advice of members of the board of the Aurea Foundation, including Mark Cameron, Andrew Coyne, Devon Cross, Allan Gotlieb, George Jonas, Margaret MacMillan, Anthony Munk, and Janice Stein.

For her contribution to the preliminary edit of the book, the debate organizers would like to thank Jane McWhinney.

Since their inception the Munk Debates have sought to take the discussions that happen at each event to national and international audiences. Here the debates have benefited immeasurably from a partnership with Canada's national newspaper, the *Globe and Mail*, and the counsel of its editor-in-chief, John Stackhouse.

With the publication of this superb book, House of Anansi Press is helping the debates reach new audiences in Canada and internationally. The debates' organizers would like to thank Anansi chair, Scott Griffin, and president and publisher, Sarah MacLachlan, for their enthusiasm for this book project and insights into how to translate the spoken debate into a powerful written intellectual exchange.

ABOUT THE DEBATERS

CHARLES KRAUTHAMMER is an American Pulitzer Prize—winning syndicated columnist, political commentator, and physician. Named by the *Financial Times* as the most influential commentator in America, Krauthammer has been honoured from every part of the political spectrum for his bold and original writing — from the famously liberal People for the American Way to the staunchly conservative Bradley Foundation. Since 1985, he has written a syndicated column for the *Washington Post* that is published weekly in more than 275 newspapers worldwide. He is also a contributing editor to *The Weekly Standard* and *The New Republic* and is a weekly panellist on *Inside Washington,* and a regular contributor on Fox's evening news program, *Special Report with Bret Baier.*

VALI NASR is an Iranian-born, renowned expert on foreign policy and on the politics and social development in the Middle East and the Muslim world. Named one of the most powerful Democrats on U.S. foreign policy by *Foreign Policy* magazine, Nasr is the dean of Johns Hopkins University's Paul H. Nitze School of Advanced International Studies in Washington, D.C. He is also a senior fellow in foreign policy at the Brookings Institution, and a member of the U.S. State Department's Foreign Policy Advisory Board.

From 2009 to 2011 Nasr served as senior adviser to the U.S. special representative for Afghanistan and Pakistan, Ambassador Richard Holbrooke. He is also the author of numerous bestselling books, including *The Shia Revival: How Conflicts within Islam Will Shape the Future*, and is a columnist for *Bloomberg View*. He is regularly consulted to provide commentary on CNN, NBC, NPR, and PBS, and has been a guest on *Larry King Live*, the *Daily Show with Jon Stewart*, and *GPS with Fareed Zakaria*.

AMOS YADLIN is a former Israeli Air Force general, Israel Defense Forces (IDF) military attaché to the United States, and head of the IDF Military Intelligence Directorate. He was one of eight pilots to successfully bomb Iraq's Osirak nuclear reactor in 1981. After retiring from the IDF in November 2010, Yadlin joined the Washington Institute for Near East Policy as the Kay Fellow on Israeli national security. In November 2011, he was appointed director of Tel Aviv University's

Institute for National Security Studies. He has written for the *New York Times*, *Foreign Affairs*, the *Wall Street Journal*, among others, and provides frequent analysis on CNN, BBC, and NPR.

FAREED ZAKARIA is host of CNN's flagship international affairs program, *Fareed Zakaria GPS*, and the editor-at-large of *Time*. He is also a *Washington Post* columnist, a *New York Times* bestselling author, and a former editor of *Newsweek International*. His most recent book, *The Post-American World*, was heralded by the *New York Times* and *The Economist*, and his previous book, *The Future of Freedom*, was a national bestseller and has been translated into over twenty languages. *Esquire* has described him as "the most influential foreign policy adviser of his generation" and, in 2010, *Foreign Policy* named him as one of the top one hundred global thinkers.

ABOUT THE EDITOR

RUDYARD GRIFFITHS is the organizer and moderator of the Munk Debates. In 2006 he was named one of Canada's "Top 40 under 40" by the *Globe and Mail*. He is the editor of thirteen books on history, politics, and international affairs, including *Who We Are: A Citizen's Manifesto*, which was a *Globe and Mail* Best Book of 2009 and a finalist for the Shaughnessy Cohen Prize for Political Writing. He lives in Toronto with his wife and two children.

ABOUT THE MUNK DEBATES

The Munk Debates are Canada's premier public policy event. Held semi-annually, the debates provide leading thinkers with a global forum to discuss the major public policy issues facing the world and Canada. Each event takes place in Toronto in front of a live audience, and the proceedings are covered by domestic and international media. Participants in recent Munk Debates include Robert Bell, Tony Blair, John Bolton, Ian Bremmer, Daniel Cohn-Bendit, Paul Collier, Howard Dean, Hernando de Soto, Gareth Evans, Mia Farrow, Niall Ferguson, William Frist, David Gratzer, Rick Hillier, Christopher Hitchens, Richard Holbrooke, Josef Joffe, Henry Kissinger, Charles Krauthammer, Paul Krugman, Lord Nigel Lawson, Stephen Lewis, David Li, Bjørn Lomborg, Lord Peter Mandelson, Elizabeth May, George Monbiot, Dambisa Moyo, Samantha Power, David Rosenberg, Lawrence Summers, and Fareed Zakaria.

The Munk Debates are a project of the Aurea Foundation, a charitable organization established in 2006 by philanthropists Peter and Melanie Munk to promote public policy research and discussion. For more information, visit www.munkdebates.com.

Has the European Experiment Failed?

Joffe and Ferguson vs. Mandelson and Cohn-Bendit

Is one of human history's most ambitious endeavours nearing collapse? Former EU Commissioner for Trade Peter Mandelson and EU Parliament co-president of the Greens/European Free Alliance Group Daniel Cohn-Bendit debate German publisher-editor and author Josef Joffe and renowned economic historian Niall Ferguson on the future of the European Union.

"For more than ten years, it has been the case that Europe has conducted an experiment in the impossible."

— Niall Ferguson

North America's Lost Decade?

Krugman and Rosenberg vs. Summers and Bremmer

The future of the North American economy is more uncertain than ever. In this edition of the Munk Debates, Nobel Prize–winning economist Paul Krugman and chief economist and strategist at Gluskin Sheff + Associates David Rosenberg square off against former U.S. Treasury Secretary Lawrence Summers and bestselling author Ian Bremmer to tackle the resolution: be it resolved North America faces a Japan-style era of high unemployment and slow growth.

"It's now impossible to deny the obvious, which is that we are not now, and have never been, on the road to recovery."

— Paul Krugman

Does the 21st Century Belong to China?
Kissinger and Zakaria vs. Ferguson and Li

Is China's rise unstoppable? Former U.S. Secretary of State Henry Kissinger and CNN's Fareed Zakaria pair off against leading historian Niall Ferguson and world-renowned Chinese economist David Daokui Li to debate China's emergence as a global force, the key geopolitical issue of our time.

This edition of the Munk Debates also features the first formal public debate Dr. Kissinger has participated in on China's future.

"I have enormous difficulty imagining a world dominated by China . . . I believe the concept that any one country will dominate the world is, in itself, a misunderstanding of the world in which we live now."

— Henry Kissinger

Hitchens vs. Blair
Christopher Hitchens vs. Tony Blair

Intellectual juggernaut and staunch atheist Christopher Hitchens goes head-to-head with former British Prime Minister Tony Blair, one of the Western world's most openly devout political leaders, on the age-old question: Is religion a force for good in the world? Few world leaders have had a greater hand in shaping current events than Blair; few writers have been more outspoken and polarizing than Hitchens.

Sharp, provocative, and thoroughly engrossing, *Hitchens vs. Blair* is a rigorous and electrifying intellectual sparring match on the contentious questions that continue to dog the topic of religion in our globalized world.

"If religious instruction were not allowed until the child had attained the age of reason, we would be living in a very different world."

— Christopher Hitchens

The Munk Debates: Volume One

Edited by Rudyard Griffiths; Introduction by Peter Munk

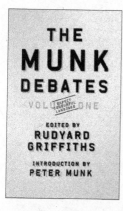

Launched in 2008 by philanthropists Peter and Melanie Munk, the Munk Debates is Canada's premier international debate series, a highly anticipated cultural event that brings together the world's brightest minds.

This volume includes the first five debates in the series, and features twenty leading thinkers and doers arguing for or against provocative resolutions that address pressing public policy concerns, such as the future of global security, the implications of humanitarian intervention, the effectiveness of foreign aid, the threat of climate change, and the state of health care in Canada and the United States.

"By trying to highlight the most important issues at crucial moments in the global conversation, these debates not only profile the ideas and solutions of some of our brightest thinkers and doers, but crystallize public passion and knowledge, helping to tackle some global challenges confronting humankind."

— Peter Munk

www.houseofanansi.com/munkdebates